Contents

To the Teacher	ii
Printing Name	1
Lowercase Alphabet	2
Uppercase Alphabet	4
Consonants	6
Short *a*	8
Short *i*	9
Short *o*	10
Practicing Short Vowels	11
Short *u*	14
Short *e*	15
Practicing Short Vowels	16
Sight Words	20
More Sight Words	21
Letter Combination *sh*	22
Letter Combination *ch*	23
Letter Combination *th*	24
Practicing Letter Combinations	25
Initial Consonant Blends	26
Vowel-Consonant-*e* Sound	28
Practicing Vowel-Consonant-*e* Sounds	32
More Sight Words	34
y Says /ī/	35
ay Says /ā/	36
ai Says /ā/	37
ow Says /ō/ and /ou/	38
oo Says /o͞o/ and /o͝o/	40
oy and *oi* Say /oi/	42
oa Says /ō/	43
ee Says /ē/	44
The *all* Words	45
c Says /k/ and /s/	46
g Says /g/ and /j/	47
aw Says /ô/	48
ea Says /ē/	49
The Ending *-ed*	50
er Says /er/	51
ar Says /ar/	52
igh Says /ī/	53
ff, *ll*, *ss* Spelling Rule	54
ld, *nd*, *st* Spelling Rule	56
k-ck Generalization	58
a After *w*	60
The Ending *-ing*	61
More Sounds to Teach	62

To the Teacher

Before using this workbook, students should work on reading readiness and letter recognition. Students should be able to name the letters of the alphabet before starting *How to Spell, 1*.

Teachers must use this workbook *with* their students. Young students who are just learning to read need supervision so that they learn the correct sounds of the vowels, consonants, blends, and letter combinations.

In its early stages, spelling is simply an outgrowth of reading. Students learn to spell by saying words and copying them. Sounds and sight words provide a good foundation for building a systematic program as young students progress in language skills.

This book can be used with an individual, with a group of students, or in a classroom. Students follow along with the teacher, taking turns as they learn the material. *All directions for students and teachers are given on each page in this book. Since students cannot read the directions, they should be told to disregard all the small print.* Their teacher will explain what they are to do on each page.

Students work individually in the workbook to reinforce what they have learned. Pages should be repeated, if necessary, until students have successfully learned the material. Then they should progress to the next lesson.

As you teach the pages with sounds and sound combinations, use the Anna Gillingham *Phonics Drill Cards*, Red Box, fifth edition. (Cambridge, Mass.: Educators Publishing Service, Inc., 1956). Take each sound card from the box as your students learn the new sound and create a current drill pack to be used in the classroom as a review drill every day.

Laura Toby Rudginsky
Elizabeth C. Haskell

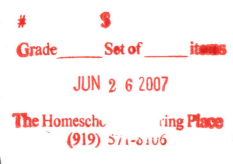

Printing Name

Print the student's first and last name. The student traces his or her name.

The student copies his or her name three times.

Lowercase Alphabet

Read the alphabet with your students. Tell them that all the letters start at the top and go down except *e*. Tell them to watch their hand position, their pencil grip, and the slant of their paper.
The students say the name of each letter as they trace the alphabet. The students say the name of each letter as they copy the alphabet.

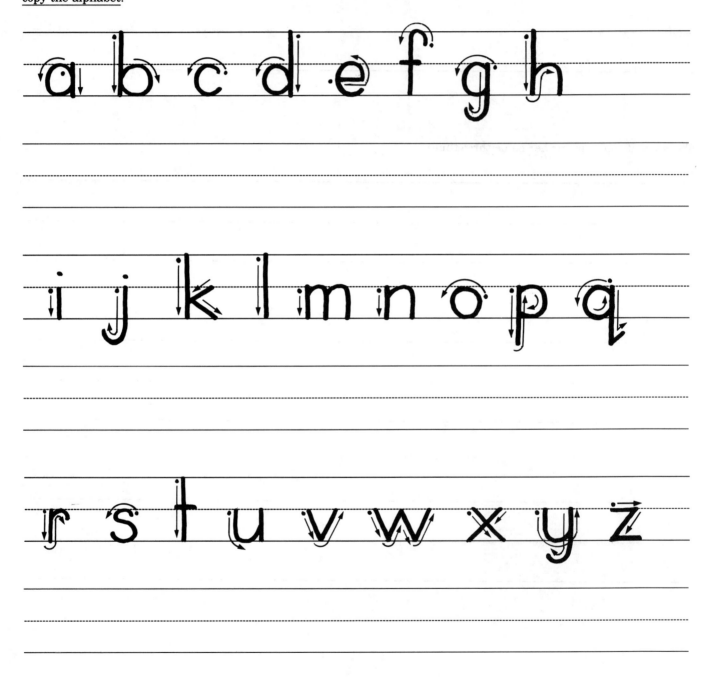

Lowercase Alphabet

The students write the alphabet.

The students write the alphabet again.

Uppercase Alphabet

If you wish your students to learn the uppercase letters at this time, read the letters with them.[1] Tell them to watch their hand position, their pencil grip, and the slant of their paper.
The students say the name of each letter as they trace the alphabet. The students say the name of each letter as they copy the alphabet.

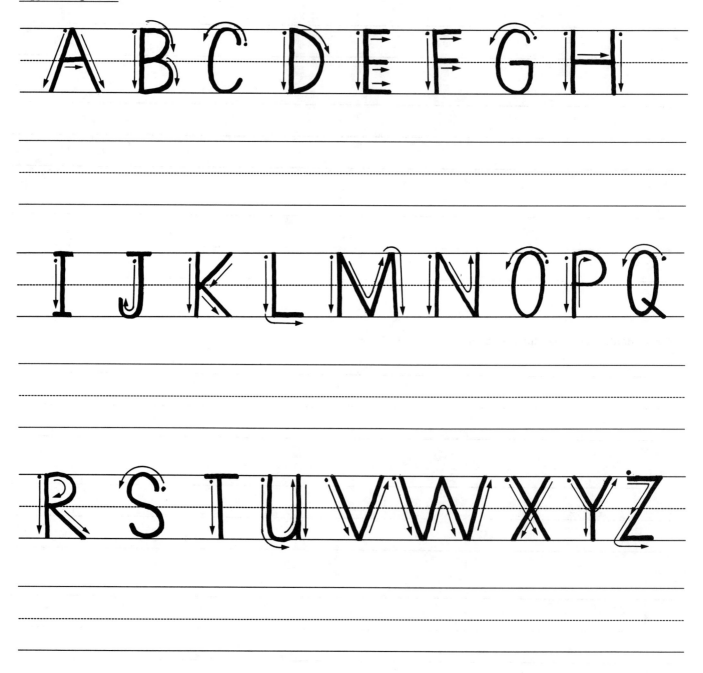

[1]Some teachers may wish to teach the uppercase letters at a later date in the year.

Uppercase Alphabet

The students write the alphabet.

The students write the alphabet again.

Consonants

Read these consonants, their sounds, and key words with your students.[1]

b says /b/ as in *bat*.

c says /k/ as in *cat*.

d says /d/ as in *dog*.

f says /f/ as in *fun*.

g says /g/ as in *go*.

h says /h/ as in *hat*.

j says /j/ as in *jam*.

k says /k/ as in *kite*.

l says /l/ as in *lamp*.

m says /m/ as in *man*.

n says /n/ as in *nut*.

---

[1] After you read this page of consonants with your students, remove the *b–n* consonant cards from the red Gillingham phonogram box. Hold up each card; each student should have a turn giving the name and sound of a consonant with its key word. Change the key word on the *b* card to *bat*.

Consonants

Read these consonants, their sounds, and key words with your students.[1]

p says /p/ as in *pan*.

q says /kw/ as in *queen*.

r says /r/ as in *rat*.

s says /s/ as in *sat*.

s says /z/ as in *has*.

t says /t/ as in *top*.

v says /v/ as in *van*.

w says /w/ as in *win*.

x says /ks/ as in *box*.

y says /y/ as in *yes*.

z says /z/ as in *zebra*.

---

[1] After you read this page of consonants with your students, remove the *p–z* consonant cards from the red Gillingham phonogram box. Hold up each card; each student should have a turn giving the name and sound of a consonant with its key word.

Short *a*

Read the vowel sound and its key word with your students. The students memorize this sentence.

a says /ă/ as in *apple*.

The students blend the sounds to make words and then read the words aloud. Add the /ă/ sound card to your classroom drill pack.

pat	hat	can	tan	cab	jab
sat	fat	pan	ran	tab	dab
mat	bat	fan	man	nab	lab

The students blend the sounds to make words, read the words aloud, and then copy the words, saying them aloud.

rat _____

Nan _____

map _____

ham _____

tan _____

cab _____

sad _____

bag _____

Dictate some of these words for the students to spell on a separate sheet of paper.

Short *i*

Read the vowel sound and its key word with your students. The students memorize this sentence.

i says /ĭ/ as in *it*.

The students blend the sounds to make words and then read the words aloud. Add the /ĭ/ sound card to your classroom drill pack.

pin	sin	big	dig	bit	pit
win	fin	jig	pig	sit	hit
tin	kin	fig	rig	fit	kit

The students blend the sounds to make words, read the words aloud, and then copy the words, saying them aloud.

dim _____   lip _____

wig _____   Tim _____

did _____   sip _____

fix _____   pin _____

Dictate some of these words for the students to spell on a separate sheet of paper.

9

Short *o*

Read the vowel sound and its key word with your students. The students memorize this sentence.

o says /ŏ/ as in *ox*.

The students blend the sounds to make words and read the words aloud. Add the /ŏ/ sound card to your classroom drill pack.

tot	got	mob	bob	dog	fog
lot	pot	sob	cob	jog	bog
hot	rot	job	rob	hog	log

The students blend the sounds to make words, read the words aloud, and then copy the words, saying them aloud.

on _____

pop _____

not _____

Tom _____

nod _____

Dot _____

hop _____

top _____

Dictate some of these words for the students to spell on a separate sheet of paper.

Practicing Short Vowels

The students sound out, read, and copy the words.

pat _____   big _____

mat _____   fig _____

fat _____   pig _____

pan _____   lot _____

tan _____   not _____

pit _____   log _____

hit _____   fog _____

Practicing Short Vowels

The students sound out, read, and copy the words.

bag _____   fit _____

sat _____   cab _____

can _____   top _____

dim _____   dog _____

Pam _____   mad _____

lit _____   ham _____

hat _____   got _____

Dictate some of these words for students to spell on a separate sheet of paper.

Practicing Short Vowels

Make up your own list of words to fit the blanks below. Tell students: "Listen to the word I say and write the missing vowel in the blank."

w__g	h__t	t__p
m__p	m__d	s__p
r__t	s__p	b__b
d__p	s__t	l__d
h__d	s__b	m__x
r__b	w__x	j__m
d__d	t__p	n__d
t__n	m__t	c__n
j__g		p__g

Dictate some of these words for the students to spell on a separate sheet of paper.

Short *u*

Read the vowel sound and its key word with your students. The students memorize this sentence.

u says /ŭ/ as in *up*.

The students blend the sounds to make words and then read the words aloud. Add the /ŭ/ sound card to your classroom drill pack.

but	jut	hug	jug	bun	gun
hut	rut	rug	lug	fun	run
nut	cut	mug	tug	sun	pun

The students blend the sounds to make words, read the words aloud, and then copy the words, saying them aloud.

up _____   us _____

mud _____   bug _____

gum _____   hum _____

tub _____   rub _____

Dictate some of these words for the students to spell on a separate sheet of paper.

Short *e*

Read the vowel sound and its key word with your students. The students memorize this sentence.

e says /ĕ/ as in *elephant*.

The students blend the sounds to make words and then read the words aloud. Add the /ĕ/ sound card to your classroom drill pack.

pen	ten	bet	met	bed	wed
den	men	get	net	fed	red
hen	Jen	let	pet	led	Ned

The students blend the sounds to make words, read the words aloud, and then copy the words, saying them aloud.

leg _____   Peg _____

yes _____   wet _____

beg _____   Meg _____

hem _____   web _____

Dictate some of these words for the students to spell on a separate sheet of paper.

Practicing Short Vowels

Read the sentences with your students.

a says /ă/ as in *apple*.   *i* says /ĭ/ as in *it*.
o says /ŏ/ as in *ox*.   *u* says /ŭ/ as in *up*.
e says /ĕ/ as in *elephant*.

The students blend the sounds to make words, read the words aloud, and then copy the words, saying them aloud.

yet _____   gum _____

fun _____   yes _____

hen _____   set _____

sun _____   Liz _____

cap _____   van _____

Dictate some of these words for the students to spell on a separate sheet of paper.

Practicing Short Vowels

Make up your own list of words to fit the blanks below. Tell students: "Listen to the word I say and write the missing vowel in the blank."

s__t	b__g	r__g
l__d	w__t	f__n
w__x	t__b	p__g
r__b	b__x	c__b
y__t	r__n	s__m
p__t	r__d	r__g
b__t	t__n	l__t
l__g	s__d	w__b
b__g		t__p

Dictate some of these words for the students to spell on a separate sheet of paper.

Practicing Short Vowels

The students make words by filling each blank with a vowel.

      a   *e*   *i*   *o*   *u*

h__t	t__n	s__t
f__t	d__d	d__g
h__m	t__p	p__t
b__t	l__t	c__b
n__t	r__n	p__n
p__p	b__g	c__t
w__g	c__p	m__p
g__t	r__d	j__g
l__p	f__n	m__t

Dictate words, phrases, and sentences from page 6 in *How to Teach Spelling* for the students to write on a separate sheet of paper.

Practicing Short Vowels

Read this story with your students. Tell them the sight words *to* and *a*.

Ted has a dog.
Ted and his dog jog.
The dog ran to a log.
Ted let his pet sit on the log.
Ted and his dog ran.
Ted and his dog had fun.

The students fill in each blank with a vowel to make a word.

a   e   i   o   u

Ted and his d__g j__g.
The dog s__t on a l__g.
Ted and his dog r__n.
Ted and his dog had f__n.

Sight Words

The students read and copy these words a few at a time. The students memorize these words a few at a time.

a _____   so _____

the _____   he _____

to _____   me _____

do _____   she _____

no _____   we _____

go _____   be _____

Dictate these words for the students to spell on a separate sheet of paper. While the students are studying these sight words, continue to review the short-vowel sounds.

More Sight Words

The students read and copy these words a few at a time. The students memorize these words a few at a time.

of

was

too

does

said

there

where

were

what

Dictate these words for the students to spell on a separate sheet of paper.

Letter Combination *sh*

Add the /sh/ sound card to your classroom drill pack. Tell the students that the letter combination *sh* may come at the beginning or end of a word. The students read and memorize this sentence.

sh says /sh/ as in *ship*.

The students blend the sounds to make words, read the words aloud, and then copy the words, saying them aloud.

shut _____   shed _____

fish _____   rash _____

shop _____   rush _____

The students read these sentences and underline all the /sh/ sounds.

The fish is in the dish.
Dash to the shed.
I wish I had a big box.
Mash the fig in the dish.

Dictate some of these words and sentences for the students to write on a separate sheet of paper. Spell the sight words *I*, *the*, and *to* for them.

Letter Combination *ch*

Add the /ch/ sound card to your classroom drill pack. Tell the students that the letter combination *ch* may come at the beginning or end of a word. The students read and memorize this sentence.

ch says /ch/ as in *chin*.

The students blend the sounds to make words, read the words aloud, and then copy the words, saying them aloud.

chip _____   such _____

bunch _____   chop _____

much _____   chat _____

The students read these sentences and underline all the /ch/ sounds.

Val is his chum.

Chop up the log.

The bench has a big chip in it.

Bev had a big lunch.

Dictate some of these words and sentences for the students to write on a separate sheet of paper.

Letter Combination *th*

Add the /th/ sound card to your classroom drill pack. Tell the students that the letter combination *th* may come at the beginning or end of a word. The students read and memorize this sentence.

th says /th/ as in *thin*.

The students blend the sounds to make words, read the words aloud, and then copy the words, saying them aloud.

that _____   then _____

them _____   than _____

this _____   thin _____

thud _____   with _____

The students read these sentences and underline all the /th/ sounds.

The dish hit the bench with a thud.
Lin has a thin fish.
That pup ran to them.

Dictate some of these words and sentences for the students to write on a separate sheet of paper.

Practicing Letter Combinations

The students read and copy these phrases.

chop that fish

get much sun

this fat pig

chat with a chum

a fish net

that thin mat

ham in a dish

Dictate these phrases for the students to write on a separate sheet of paper.

Initial Consonant Blends

The students read these blends aloud. The students read and copy these blends with a key word.

bl	blot	
cl	club	
fl	flag	
gl	glad	
pl	plan	
sl	sled	
sp	spot	
st	stop	
sw	swim	
sm	smog	
sn	snap	

Initial Consonant Blends

The students read these blends aloud. The students read and copy these blends with a key word.

br _____   brag _____

cr _____   crib _____

dr _____   drip _____

fr _____   frog _____

gr _____   grab _____

pr _____   prop _____

tr _____   trip _____

sc _____   scab _____

sk _____   skip _____

tw _____   twin _____

Dictate words with initial consonant blends from pages 17 through 22 in *How to Teach Spelling* for the students to write on a separate sheet of paper.
When dictating the /k/ sound, tell the students whether to spell it with *c* or *k*.

Vowel-Consonant-*e* Sound

Read the following with your students.

> The *e* at the end of a word is silent.
> The vowel before the silent *e* has a long sound. The vowel says its own name.
> There must be one consonant between the vowel and the silent *e*.

The students memorize these sentences.

a-consonant-*e* says /ā/ as in *safe*.
e-consonant-*e* says /ē/ as in *these*.
i-consonant-*e* says /ī/ as in *pine*.

After you read these vowel-consonant-*e* sounds with your students, remove the vowel-consonant-*e* cards from the red Gillingham phonogram box. Hold up each card; each student has a turn giving the name and sound of the vowel-consonant-*e* phonogram with its key word. Add these cards to your classroom drill pack.

Vowel-Consonant-*e* Sound

Read each word with your students. The students copy the word and add an *e* to the end of it. Then the students read the new word aloud.

Word	Vowel-Consonant-*e* Word
mad	
can	
hid	
cap	
bit	
rid	
pin	
dim	
hat	

Vowel-Consonant-*e* Sound

Read the following with your students.

> The *e* at the end of a word is silent.
>
> The vowel before the silent *e* has a long sound. The vowel says its own name.
>
> There must be one consonant between the vowel and the silent *e*.

The students memorize these sentences.

> *o*-consonant-*e* says /ō/ as in *home*.
>
> *u*-consonant-*e* says /ū/ as in *mule*.

After you read these vowel-consonant-*e* sounds with your students, remove the vowel-consonant-*e* card from the red Gillingham phonogram box. Hold up each card; each student has a turn giving the name and sound of the vowel-consonant-*e* phonogram with its key word. Add these cards to your classroom drill pack. Using the phonogram cards, review all the vowel-consonant-*e* sounds.

Vowel-Consonant-*e* Sound

Read each word with your students. The students copy the word and add an *e* to the end of it. Then the students read the new word aloud.

Word	Vowel-Consonant-*e* Word
cut	
hop	
bit	
fad	
rob	
rod	
fin	
mop	
tub	

Practicing Vowel-Consonant-*e* Sounds

The students read the short-vowel word and then the corresponding vowel-consonant-*e* word. Remind them that the silent *e* at the end of the word changes the sound of the vowel.

at — ate   fin — fine

us — use   hat — hate

mad — made   rat — rate

dim — dime   win — wine

rid — ride   rip — ripe

hop — hope   man — mane

cod — code   tub — tube

can — cane   rod — rode

bit — bite   cub — cube

cut — cute   not — note

Practicing Vowel-Consonant-*e* Sounds

Read these phrases with your students. The students copy the phrases.

save the whale

ride the mule

fire sale

late date

hole in the tire

nine and five

same time

hide the dime

Dictate some of these phrases for the students to write on a separate sheet of paper. When dictating the /k/ sound, tell the students whether to spell it with *c* or *k*.

More Sight Words

The students read and copy these words. Then the students memorize these words.

want _____

have _____

some _____

come _____

are _____

you _____

your _____

says _____

goes _____

Dictate these words for the students to spell on a separate sheet of paper. Then dictate the sentences that include all the sight words on page 33 in *How to Teach Spelling*.

y Says /ī/

The students read, copy, and memorize these words.

my _____   fly _____

by _____   spy _____

cry _____   try _____

dry _____   shy _____

The students read and copy these phrases.

fry the egg _____

try my bike _____

a shy fly _____

the sly fox _____

cloth is dry _____

Dictate these phrases for the students to spell on a separate sheet of paper. When dictating the /k/ sound, tell the students whether to spell it with *c* or *k*.

ay Says /ā/

Read this vowel combination and its key word with your students.
Add the *ay* phonics card to your classroom drill pack. The students memorize this sentence.

ay says /ā/ as in *play* at the end of a word.

The students read these words aloud, underlining *ay* as they say the words.

| may | hay | pay | ray |
| say | day | gay | lay |

The students say each letter as they copy the word. Then they read the word aloud.

clay _____   play _____

stay _____   bay   _____

way   _____   bray _____

tray _____   slay _____

sway _____   gray _____

Dictate these words for the students to spell on a separate sheet of paper. When dictating words with the /k/ sound, tell the students whether to spell it with *c* or *k*.

ai Says /ā/

Read this vowel combination and its key word with your students.
Add the *ai* phonics card to your classroom drill pack.
The students memorize this sentence.

ai says /ā/ as in *sail* at the beginning or in the middle of a word.

The students read these words aloud, underlining *ai* as they say the words.

ail	paid	aid	maid
mail	tail	wait	train

The students say each letter as they copy the word. Then they read the word aloud.

rain _____ main _____

pain _____ gain _____

jail _____ nail _____

aim _____ fail _____

trail _____ braid _____

Dictate these words for the students to spell on a separate sheet of paper.

ow Says /ō/ and /ou/

Read these vowel combinations and their key words with your students.
Add the *ow* phonics card to your classroom drill pack.
The students memorize these sentences.

ow says /ō/ as in *snow*.
ow says /ou/ as in *plow*.

The students read these words aloud, underlining *ow* as they say the words. Then they copy the words.

ow says /ō/	*ow* says /ou/
grow	how
show	now
snow	cow
own	owl
low	plow
blow	brow
flow	town
row	down

ow Says /ō/ and /ou/

Ask the students to read these words. Ask them which sound of *ow* each word has. Have them try both sounds. If a word does not sound like a word they know, then they must try the other sound. The students copy these words.

crow	own
down	brow
cow	growl
mow	grow
clown	howl
owl	gown
brown	row
show	town
flow	slow

oo Says /o͞o/ and /o͝o/

Read these vowel combinations and their key words with your students.
Add the *oo* phonics card to your classroom drill pack.
The students memorize these sentences.

oo says /o͞o/ as in *food*.
oo says /o͝o/ as in *book*.

The students read these words aloud, underlining *oo* as they say the words. Then they copy the words.

oo says /o͞o/

oo says /o͝o/

food	book
moon	look
room	wool
broom	foot
soon	stood
tooth	shook
proof	wood
pool	brook

oo Says /o͞o/ and /o͝o/

Ask the students to read these words. Ask them which sound of *oo* each word has. Have them try both sounds. If a word does not sound like a word they know, then they must try the other sound. The students copy these words.

foot	hood
shook	took
food	boot
moon	proof
good	shoot
wool	broom
look	book
pool	smooth
tooth	spoon

oy and *oi* Say /oi/

Read these vowel combinations and their key words with your students.
Add these phonics cards to your classroom drill pack.
The students memorize these sentences.

oy says /oi/ as in *toy* at the end of a word.

oi says /oi/ as in *oil* and *boil* at the beginning or in the middle of a word.

The students read these words aloud, copy them, and underline the /oi/ sound.

boy _____   Joy _____

toy _____   Roy _____

oil _____   join _____

boil _____   joint _____

soil _____   point _____

spoil _____ noise _____

oa Says /ō/

Read this vowel combination and its key word with your students.
Add the *oa* phonics card to your classroom drill pack.[1]
The students memorize this sentence.

oa says /ō/ as in *boat*.

The students read these words aloud, underlining *oa* as they say the words.

oak	coat	toad	soak
road	coal	foam	goal
float			loaf

The students say each letter as they copy the word. Then they read the word aloud.

groan _____ boast _____

load _____ coast _____

soap _____ roast _____

goat _____ toast _____

coach _____ loan _____

Dictate these words for the students to spell on a separate sheet of paper. When dictating words with the /k/ sound, tell the students whether to spell it with *c* or *k*.

[1] There are a few words in which *oe* says /ō/. Teach your students this sound using the *oe* phonics card and teach them the words *Joe* and *toe*.

ee Says /ē/

Read this vowel combination and its key word with your students.
Add the *ee* phonics card to your classroom drill pack.
The students memorize this sentence.

ee says /ē/ as in *feed*.

The students read the words aloud, underlining *ee* as they say the words.

feed	feet	meet	week
see	free	sleep	seem
tree			weed

The students say each letter as they copy the word. Then they read the word aloud.

need	_____	deep	_____
keep	_____	green	_____
seed	_____	seen	_____
heel	_____	sheep	_____
sweet	_____	beef	_____
feel	_____	sweep	_____

Dictate these words for the students to spell on a separate sheet of paper. When dictating words with the /k/ sound, tell the students whether to spell it with *c* or *k*.

The *all* Words

Read these words with your students. The students read the words aloud, copying them as they say them.

all _____   tall _____

call _____   mall _____

fall _____   wall _____

ball _____   small _____

hall _____   stall _____

The students fill in the blanks with one of the words listed above.

Bat the _____.

Shop at the _____.

Pat is big and _____.

My chum had a bad _____.

Did she _____ you?

c Says /k/ and /s/

Read the sounds of this consonant with your students.[1] The students memorize these sentences.

c says /k/ as in *cat*.

c says /s/ when it comes before *e*, *i*, or *y*.

Read these words aloud with your students. The students copy the words and then read them.

cat	_____	city	_____
cot	_____	cent	_____
cut	_____	cyclone	_____
clap	_____	ice	_____
crow	_____	rice	_____
crab	_____	nice	_____
cob	_____	slice	_____

[1] It is not necessary for first-grade students to know the spelling of all these words. The point of this exercise is for the students to learn both sounds of *c*. Now when your students respond to the *c* phonics card, have them give both sounds.

46

g Says /g/ and /j/

Read the sounds of this consonant with your students.[1] The students memorize these sentences.

g says /g/ as in *go*.
g usually says /j/ when it comes before *e*, *i*, or *y*.

Read these words aloud with your students. The students copy the words and then read them.[2]

gum   gym

gas   cage

gust   gem

grab   stage

got   age

gun   hinge

glad   page

[1] Teach these words as exceptions: *get*, *girl*, *give*, and *gift*.
[2] It is not necessary for first-grade students to know the spelling of all these words. The point of this exercise is for the students to learn both sounds of *g*. Now when your students respond to the *g* phonics card, have them give both sounds.

aw Says /ô/

Read this vowel combination and its key word with your students.[1]
Add the *aw* phonics card to your classroom drill pack.
The students memorize this sentence.

aw says /ô/ as in *saw*.

The students read the words aloud, underlining *aw* as they say the words.

jaw	lawn
law	dawn
raw	draw
paw	thaw
claw	yawn

The students fill in the blanks with *aw*. Then they read the words aloud.

h____k   y____n

d____n   l____n

sh____l   b____l

cr____l   dr____n

[1] It is not necessary for first-grade students to know the spelling of all these words. The point of this exercise is for the students to learn the sound of *aw*.

ea Says /ē/

Read this vowel combination and its key word with your students.[1]
Add the *ea* phonics card to your classroom drill pack.
The students memorize this sentence.

ea says /ē/ as in *eat*.

The students read the words aloud, underlining *ea* as they say the words.

meat	steal	seal	team
seat	beach	meal	leaf
heat	peach	read	cheat

The students say each letter as they copy the word. Then they read the word aloud.

cream _____   neat _____

each _____   sneak _____

dream _____   bead _____

clean _____   teach _____

reach _____   lead _____

[1]Teach your students to read these words:

/ā/	/ĕ/
great	bread
steak	read
break	head

The Ending -ed

Add the *ed* phonics card to your classroom drill pack.
The students read and memorize these sentences.

ed says /ed/ as in *rented*.
ed says /d/ as in *sailed*.
ed says /t/ as in *jumped*.

The students add *ed* to these words. The students read the words, emphasizing the sound *ed* has at the end of each word.

snow____   help____   mail____

land____   bump____   sand____

hunt____   wish____   mash____

rust____   dent____   brush____

plow____   rest____   dust____

leak____   limp____   dream____

yawn____   boast____   crawl____

er Says /er/

Add the *er* phonics card to your classroom drill pack.
The students read and memorize this sentence.

er says /er/ as in *her*.

The students read these words aloud, underlining *er* as they say the words.

perch	jerk	fern	term
stern	cooler	her	golfer
hunter	sander	player	taller
sifter	painter	cleaner	smaller
greener	deeper	winter	helper
dreamer	bumper	sweeter	reader

ar Says /ar/

Add the *ar* phonics card to your classroom drill pack.
The students read and memorize this sentence.

ar says /ar/ as in *car*.

The students read these words aloud, copy them, and learn to spell them.

star

jar

bar

tar

far

yard

start

part

The students read and copy these phrases.

scar on her arm

park the car

barn on the farm

star in the sky

Dictate these words and phrases for the students to write on a separate sheet of paper. When dictating the /k/ sound, tell the students whether to spell it with *c* or *k*.

igh Says /ī/

Add the *igh* phonics card to your classroom drill pack.
The students read and memorize this sentence.

igh says /ī/ as in *light*.

The students read these words aloud, copy them, and learn to spell them.

high

sigh

might

sight

bright

fight

tight

flight

The students read and copy these phrases.

bright light

a dark night

the high wall

his right hand

Dictate these words and phrases for the students to write on a separate sheet of paper.

ff, *ll*, *ss* Spelling Rule

Read this spelling rule with your students. The students memorize this rule.

One-syllable words that end in *f*, *l*, or *s* almost always double the *f*, *l*, or *s*.

Read these words with your students.

puff	bell	miss
huff	fell	kiss
cuff	tell	mess
off	kill	less
whiff	fill	grass
stiff	will	dress
gruff	spill	pass
stuff	still	fuss
muff	grill	cross
staff	spell	loss
sniff	doll	class

The words below are exceptions to the *ff*, *ll*, *ss* Spelling Rule. Read them with your students. The students memorize them.

if	pal	us
elf		bus
		yes
		gas
		this
		Gus

ff, *ll*, *ss* Spelling Rule

The students read these words aloud, copy them, and learn to spell them.

ff		**ss**	
puff		miss	
huff		kiss	
off		less	
stiff		dress	
gruff		grass	
stuff		glass	
ll		**Exceptions**	
bell		if	
fell		elf	
spill		pal	
spell		gas	
doll		yes	
will		this	

Dictate these words for the students to spell on a separate sheet of paper. Also dictate some of the phrases and sentences from page 35 in *How to Teach Spelling*. When dictating the /k/ sound, tell the students whether to spell it with *c* or *k*.

ld, *nd*, *st* Spelling Rule

When *i* and *o* come before *ld*, *nd*, and *st*, they sometimes have their long sound (they say their own names).

Read these words aloud with your students. The students copy these words and learn to spell them.

ld

old
cold
fold
gold
hold
sold
told
child
mild
wild

nd

bind
find
kind
mind
wind

st

host
most
post
ghost

Dictate these words for the students to spell on a separate sheet of paper. Dictate some of the phrases and sentences from page 36 in *How to Teach Spelling*. When dictating the /k/ sound, tell the students whether to spell it with *c* or *k*.

ld, nd, st **Spelling Rule**

The students read and copy these phrases.

kind old man

a blind child

a mild day

sold the most

had a cold

find the gold

hold the post

fold the cloth

a bold ghost

mold the clay

wind up the car

k-ck Generalization

Read this lesson with your students. This lesson teaches them when to use *k* or *ck* at the end of a word.

Both *k* and *ck* say /k/.
Use *ck* right after a single short vowel.
Use *k* after a consonant (*milk*),
after a long-vowel sound (*bake*),
and after two vowels (*look*).

The students write the following words in the correct column.

bank	back	pick	make	luck	pink
book	clock	take	check	trick	sank
park					speck

_____ *k* _____   _____ *ck* _____

k-ck Generalization

The students write *k* or *ck* in the blanks. Then they write the words and read them aloud.

k or ck

in___   ___   loo___   ___

hun___   ___   tan___   ___

ta___e   ___   clo___   ___

blin___   ___   span___   ___

cli___   ___   po___e   ___

lu___   ___   tri___   ___

par___   ___   tra___   ___

drin___   ___   chun___   ___

stu___   ___   rin___   ___

pa___   ___   che___   ___

Dictate some of the words, phrases, and sentences from the lists on pages 39–41 in *How to Teach Spelling*.

a After *w*

Read this sentence with your students. The students memorize it.

An *a* after *w* says /ô/.

Read these words aloud with your students. The students copy and learn to spell them.

war   wad

want   swamp

swap   swan

wand   wash

wander   water

The students read and copy these phrases.

swat the wasp

wave the wand

wad of gum

want some milk

water the plant

Dictate these words and phrases for the students to write on a separate sheet of paper.

The Ending -*ing*

Read this lesson with your students. The students memorize it.

The Ending -ing

When you add *ing* to a word that ends in silent *e*, drop the *e* and add *ing*.

like + ing = liking

When you add *ing* to a word that doesn't end in silent *e*, just add *ing*.

go + ing = going

The students write the words and add *ing*. Remind the students to drop the silent *e* before they add *ing*.

save + ing = _____

do + ing = _____

race + ing = _____

care + ing = _____

box + ing = _____

want + ing = _____

Dictate these words for the students to spell on a separate sheet of paper. Remind the students to drop the silent *e* before adding *ing*. When dictating the /k/ sound, tell the students whether to spell it with *c* or *k*.

More Sounds to Teach

Teach your students the following sounds by adding the corresponding cards one at a time to your classroom drill pack. Use this drill pack for review.

wh says /hw/ as in *white*.

qu says /kw/ as in *queen*.

ph says /f/ as in *phone*.

au says /ô/ as in *August*.

ie says /ē/ as in *chief*.

ie says /ī/ as in *pie*.[1]

ew says /ū/ as in *few*.

ue says /o͞o/ as in *true*.[2]

eigh says /ā/ as in *eight*.

ey says /ē/ as in *key*.

ey says /ā/ as in *they*.[3]

ir says /er/ as in *bird*.

ur says /er/ as in *burn*.

u says /o͝o/ in *put*, *pull*, and *push*.

[1] Use *pie* as the key word for the /ī/ sound on the *ie* phonics card. Do not use *Billie*.
[2] For first-grade students, use only the /o͞o/ sound for *ue*.
[3] Add this sound to the *ey* phonics drill card.